EXPLORE
SOIL!

Kathleen M. Reilly

Illustrated by Bryan Stone

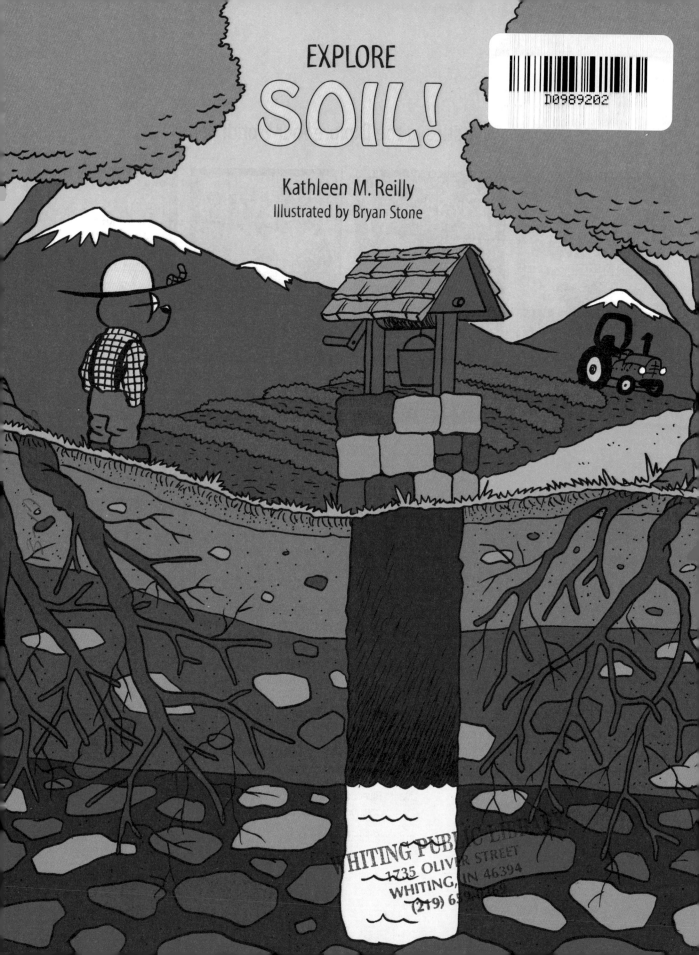

Newest titles in the **Explore Your World!** Series

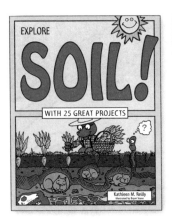

Check out more titles at www.nomadpress.net

Nomad Press
A division of Nomad Communications
10 9 8 7 6 5 4 3 2 1

This book was manufactured by Marquis Book Printing,
Montmagny, Québec, Canada
September 2015, Job #115306

ISBN Softcover: 978-1-61930-295-2
ISBN Hardcover: 978-1-61930-296-9

Illustrations by Bryan Stone
Educational Consultant, Marla Conn

Questions regarding the ordering of this book should be addressed to
Nomad Press
2456 Christian St.
White River Junction, VT 05001
www.nomadpress.net

Printed in Canada.

CONTENTS

Interested in primary sources? Look for this icon.
Use a smartphone or tablet app to scan the QR code and explore more!
You can find a list of URLs on the Resources page.

If the QR code doesn't work, try searching the Internet
with the Keyword Prompts to find other helpful sources.

KEYWORD PROMPTS

keep soil healthy

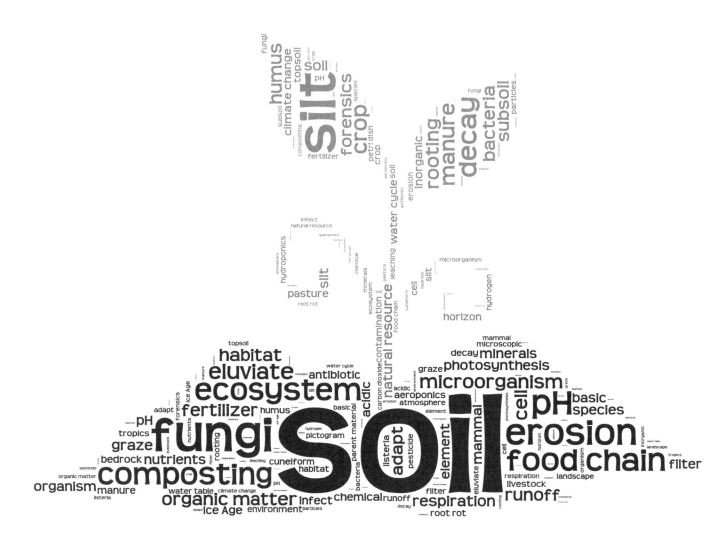

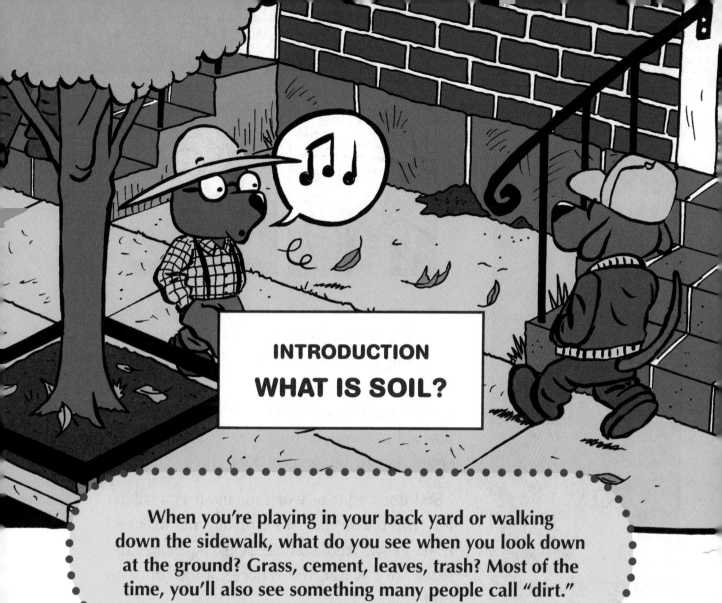

INTRODUCTION
WHAT IS SOIL?

When you're playing in your back yard or walking down the sidewalk, what do you see when you look down at the ground? Grass, cement, leaves, trash? Most of the time, you'll also see something many people call "dirt."

WORDS to KNOW

soil: the top layer of the earth, in which plants grow.

natural resource: something from nature that people can use in some way, such as water, stone, and wood.

You might think, "What's the big deal about dirt? It's everywhere." That dirt is actually soil, which is very important to life on Earth. It's one of the three most important natural resources on our planet, along with air and water. Without soil, there wouldn't be life on Earth.

WORDS to KNOW

habitat: a plant or animal's home.

organism: a living thing.

nutrients: substances in food, soil, and air that living things need to live and grow.

substance: the material that something is made of.

organic matter: rotting plants and animals that give soil its nutrients.

organic: something that is or was living.

inorganic: not living.

particle: a tiny piece of matter.

silt: particles of fine soil, rich in nutrients.

WORDS to KNOW

In the same way that you have skin covering your whole body, our planet has soil covering its entire surface. Soil covers the ground in natural places, such as meadows, gardens, forests, and your back yard. Some places have only a thin layer of soil. In other spots, it can be several feet thick.

Soil does a lot of work for us. It is a habitat for tiny organisms. Most of our plants need it to grow. And soil recycles nutrients and filters our water, too. There's a lot going on under your feet!

WHAT'S IN SOIL?

Soil is made up of lots of different materials. The organic matter in soil includes little bits of dead plants and animals. There are tiny bits of inorganic matter, too, such as broken-down rocks and pebbles. There are also even smaller particles in soil, such as sand, silt, and clay.

Did You Know?

Dirt isn't the same as soil. Dirt is soil that's no longer useful or wanted, such as the dirt under your fingernails or on the floor.

2

Sand is the largest particle you'll find in soil. Have you ever scooped up a handful of soil at the beach and looked at it closely? You'll be able to see each little grain of sand.

Silt particles are smaller than sand. If you drag your hand lightly along the bottom of a running stream, you can snag a little bit of soil that's being carried along with the current. If you look at it very closely, you might be able to see individual particles—but they're really small!

Clay is made of the smallest particles. You won't be able to see the individual particles just by looking at a lump of clay. You need a microscope to see them because they're so small. When clay particles get wet, they turn really sticky and clump together. Have you ever played with clay?

Squeezed between all these soil particles are air and water. That's how plants grow in soil—they push their roots between the particles to get the water and nutrients they need.

3

THE FIRST STEP

Rocks are very hard. If you drop one on your foot, it hurts! But they can be broken into smaller pieces under the right conditions. That's how soil starts.

Rock is called the parent material of soil because it's where most soil comes from. Soil comes from the parent material of rock just as you come from your parent! Water, ice, and wind break down bedrock through time.

Water can move forcefully enough to push rocks, tumble them around, and knock them into each other. As the water continues to roll them, little pieces break off, and then they start tumbling around, too. In time, the pieces get smaller and smaller.

Did You Know?

The largest particle of clay is 500 times smaller than a single grain of sand!

SLIP-SLIDING AWAY

There are some locations where soil can't form. Have you ever seen craggy mountain peaks? They are often bare, just peaks of exposed rocks. That's because gravity pulls any soil-making materials, such as sand particles and organic matter, down the sides before any layer of soil has a chance to form. Water and wind wash materials down from mountaintops, too.

4

Ice can break down rocks, too. Rainwater seeps into cracks in the bedrock. When the water freezes, it expands. This forces the cracks to get wider and wider, sometimes splitting the entire rock into smaller pieces.

Wind wears away rocks by blowing small particles such as grains of sand against them. This grinds down the rock, just as when you rub sandpaper against a piece of wood. All these little particles of rock become part of the soil.

expand: to spread out and take up more space.

decay: to break down and rot.

bacteria: tiny organisms found in animals, plants, soil, and water.

fungi: organisms that grow on and feed on rotting things.

microscopic: something so small that it can be seen only with a microscope.

WORDS to KNOW

A LITTLE BIT OF THIS AND THAT

Rock particles aren't the only things in soil. When plants and animals die, they decay, or rot. Bacteria and fungi help this organic matter break down.

Bacteria are microscopic living things that are too small to see with your eyes—but they have a very big job. You have some kinds of bacteria in your mouth and digestive system to help you digest your food.

humus: soil formed from decaying leaves and organisms.

WORDS to **KNOW**

Maybe you've seen mold when an old piece of bread has started to grow something green and fuzzy on it. That's fungi! Fungi include mold and mushrooms.

Bacteria and fungi work hard to break down dead plants and animals into tiny pieces called humus. Humus is very dark brown or black, moist, and extremely rich in nutrients.

The particles in soil might be small, but there's still room for air to fit around them. This air helps the creatures that live in the soil, such as earthworms, move around. Earthworms leave more air space in the holes they leave behind. These spaces allow plants to push their roots through the soil.

Soil is also made of water. Just as the air fills in the empty spaces, water does too. It gets absorbed by some of the material in soil and moves around to fill any empty pockets, carrying nutrients as it goes.

Soil isn't the same all over the planet, though. Think about the desert. Because there isn't much water, there aren't as many plants or animals living in the desert, so the soil there has less humus from decaying organic matter. A prairie has a lot of plants and animals, so it's far richer in humus.

Just for FUN!

WHAT DO YOU GET WHEN YOU CROSS DIRT WITH A DOG?
A Land Rover!

There are more than 50,000 different types of soil in the United States! That's because there are different kinds of rocks, organisms, land features, and weather conditions all across the country. What lives in the soil in your yard? Let's find out!

Did You Know?

Prairies are areas covered in grassland. They have most of the earth's soil—21.5 percent. Areas near active volcanoes, where there's a lot of volcanic ash, have the least—only 0.7 percent!

GOOD SCIENCE PRACTICES

Every good scientist keeps a science journal! Choose a notebook to use as your science journal. As you read through this book and do the activities, keep track of your observations and record each step in a scientific method worksheet, like the one shown here. Scientists use the scientific method to keep their experiments organized.

Each chapter of this book begins with an essential question to help guide your exploration of soil.

Question: What are we trying to find out? What problem are we trying to solve?
Research: What do other people think?
Hypothesis/Prediction: What do we think the answer will be?
Equipment: What supplies are we using?
Method: What procedure are we following?
Results: What happened and why?

? ESSENTIAL QUESTION

Keep the question in your mind as you read the chapter. At the end of each chapter, use your science journal to record your thoughts and answers.

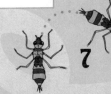

PAINT WITH SOIL

Soil from different locations can be different colors, depending on what it's made of. Since ancient times, soil has been used for painting. You, too, can create works of art with soil!

1 Put one soil sample at a time on a piece of paper and use the hammer or mallet to crush it into very small pieces. **Wear goggles for safety!**

2 Put the pieces into a plastic Ziploc bag and use the rolling pin to crush it into a very fine powder. If you have a mortar and pestle, you can grind it into a powder that way. Repeat with all of your samples until they are all very fine powders. Keep them separate!

3 Place one soil powder sample into a paper cup. Stretch the pantyhose over the top of the cup and shake the cup over a new piece of paper or a paper plate. You're going to end up with a super-fine powder on your paper to use as a base for your paint. Repeat with the other colors on separate pieces of paper. When you're finished, put each colored powder into a new paper cup.

SUPPLIES

- ✿ several dry soil samples from different places, about ¼ cup each
- ✿ several pieces of paper
- ✿ goggles
- ✿ hammer or mallet
- ✿ plastic Ziploc bags
- ✿ rolling pin or mortar and pestle
- ✿ paper cups
- ✿ small section of old pantyhose
- ✿ paper plates
- ✿ marker or pen
- ✿ tape
- ✿ clear acrylic artist paint (you can use white paint or even just water)
- ✿ small artist paint brush or old bits of sponge or rag

(PS) **These famous cave paintings in Lascaux, France, were made with soil.** They have survived for more than 17,000 years! How are they different from paintings you see on the walls of museums?

KEYWORD PROMPTS

Lascaux cave painting 🔍

topsoil: the top layer of soil.

4 On another piece of paper, sketch out a drawing with your marker or pen. You can skip this step if you want to just start painting! Use the tape to secure your paper flat to the surface you're working on. It will need to stay very still until it's done drying.

Did You Know?

Soil formation doesn't happen overnight, or even in a week, a month, or a whole year. In some places, it can take more than 500 years to form an inch of **topsoil!**

5 Add a small bit of clear paint to each color of powdered soil and mix until they're at the consistency of paint. If you're using water, get your sponge or paintbrush wet and dip it in the powder.

6 Begin painting! When you're finished, let the painting stay flat and undisturbed until it's dry.

TRY THIS! Mix your powder and clear paint into different consistencies. Does a thinner mixture look different on paper? How? How do the different colors and consistencies look when they've dried?

ANALYZE SOIL

You might live in an area that has a lot of sand mixed in with the soil. Or maybe most of the soil around you looks like thick, red clay. With this project, you can find out what's in your soil. Start a scientific method worksheet to organize your ideas and observations.

1 In your yard or a nearby field, scoop up about a cup of soil and put it in your container.

2 Fill your jar about halfway with water. Add the soil to the jar, cover, and shake well. Then put the jar in a place where it won't be disturbed and watch what happens as the soil settles. Which particles do you think will reach the bottom of the jar first, the large ones or the small ones?

3 Check your jar after 1 minute, 30 minutes, and an entire day. Does it look different every time? Do you see layers forming in the soil that settles on the bottom of the jar? Record your observations in your science journal. Draw a picture of the layers you see in your jar. Look at the picture here to discover what each layer is made of.

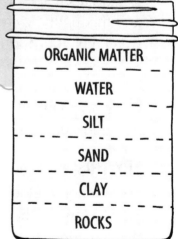

ORGANIC MATTER

WATER

SILT

SAND

CLAY

ROCKS

4 Different areas in your own neighborhood might have different soil. Collect small samples from other areas, such as near a pond or in a garden. Be sure to get permission before scooping up someone's property, though!

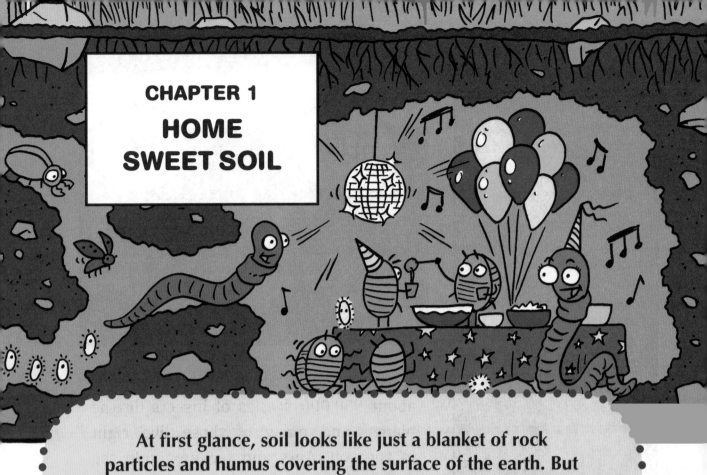

CHAPTER 1
HOME SWEET SOIL

At first glance, soil looks like just a blanket of rock particles and humus covering the surface of the earth. But there's more to soil than you think! It's home to all kinds of living things. In fact, in one teaspoon of soil, there can be billions of **microbes**, plus many different insects!

Have you noticed the earthworms that live in the soil? Earthworms are perfectly suited to their life there. When they wiggle through the soil, earthworms make tiny tunnels that help let in air and water. But they also move soil around, mixing and moving the nutrients. They eat tiny bits of dead leaves and other organic materials, breaking it down even more so plants can use it.

WORDS to KNOW

microbe: a tiny living or nonliving thing. Bacteria and fungi are living microbes that are also called microorganisms.

? ESSENTIAL QUESTION

What does soil provide for the organisms that live in it?

WORDS to KNOW

species: a group of plants or animals that are related and look like each other.

cell: the smallest, most basic part of a living thing.

tropics: the area near the equator. This is the imaginary line around the earth halfway between the North and South Poles.

mammal: a warm-blooded animal, such as a human, dog, or cat, that can keep itself warm. Mammals feed milk to their young and usually have hair or fur covering most of their skin.

WORDS to KNOW

Insects live in the soil, too. There are about 950,000 species of insects on the planet, and many of those live right in the soil. Ants and termites rule the underground world. Some other soil-dwelling insects include potato bugs, woodlice, millipedes, beetles, slugs, snails, and mites.

The fungi and bacteria that live in soil do similar jobs—they help break down organic materials into soil. But they are different in a couple of ways. Bacteria are usually smaller in size, but there are more bacteria than fungi. And bacteria are made up of one cell. Most fungi are made of many cells. What about you? Are you made of one cell or many cells?

Did You Know?

Ants are one of the world's most abundant insects. If you weighed all the ants that live in just the tropics, they would weigh more than all of the mammals combined.

12

MORE SOIL RESIDENTS

Larger creatures live in the soil, too, including moles. Moles live underground all the time, and they are perfectly made for it. They have tiny eyes, velvety fur, and big, flipper-like paws to dig and push at the earth. They eat earthworms and grubs. Other creatures, such as prairie dogs and chipmunks, make their homes underground but come above ground to find food.

WORDS to KNOW

landscape: a large area of land with specific features.

acidic: describes a substance that is low on the pH scale and loses hydrogen in water. Examples of acidic substances include lemon juice and vinegar.

basic: describes a substance that is high on the pH scale and gains hydrogen in water. Examples of basic substances include soap, baking soda, and ammonia.

chemical: the pure form of a substance. It has certain features that can react with other substances. Some chemicals can be combined or broken up to create new chemicals.

SOIL AND PH

Different parts of the planet have different kinds of rocks, organisms, landscapes, and weather conditions. This means that the soil in different parts of the world is different.

Not all organisms can live in all types of soil. Some organisms need soil that is acidic and some organisms need soil that is basic.

Different substances are made of different chemicals. Scientists look at how a substance interacts with water to figure out how acidic it is.

WORDS to KNOW

hydrogen: the most common **element** in the universe. Hydrogen and oxygen are the two elements in water.

element: a pure substance that can't be broken down, such as hydrogen, oxygen, carbon, or gold.

pH: the scale people use to measure how acidic or basic something is.

Water is made up of hydrogen and oxygen. If a substance interacts with water and produces more hydrogen, it's considered to be an acid. Substances are measured by a scale to show how acidic or basic they are. The scale goes from 1 to 14 and uses a measurement called pH.

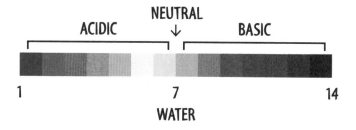

ACIDIC   NEUTRAL   BASIC
↓
1   7   14
WATER

Substances measuring between 1 and 7 on the pH scale are acidic. They have a low pH. Substances that measure between 7 and 14 are basic. They have a high pH. Pure water is neutral and has a pH of 7, right in the middle.

pH 5

pH 8

WHICH PH FOR PLANTS?

Most plants do best in slightly acidic soil that has a pH between 5 and 7. But some plants, such as blueberries, do well in more acidic soil with a pH between 4 and 5. Other plants, such as cactuses, prefer to grow in soil that's higher on the pH scale. A pH of higher than 7 is called basic or alkaline.

MATTER MATTERS!

Everything, even you, is made up of matter. Matter is made of tiny particles called atoms. When atoms join together, they form clusters called molecules. Imagine that atoms are like letters and molecules are like words. A group of atoms joins together to make a molecule just like a group of letters joins together to make a word.

An element is a substance that's made of just one type of atom. Gold, hydrogen, and oxygen are all examples of elements. Sometimes atoms from different elements combine to make compounds. Water is a compound made of hydrogen and oxygen atoms.

(PS) **Scientists arrange elements in a periodic table.** You can look at one here!

KEYWORD PROMPTS

kids periodic table 🔍

Soil is measured on this scale, too. Why is it important to know the pH of soil? Because different plants are adapted to using different nutrients and chemicals in the soil. Also, the bacteria that help the plants grow thrive in different pH levels, too.

Soil is an amazing resource that most people don't think about very often. In this book, you'll learn why soil is so important to our planet. Let's explore the dangers our soil faces and how you can help keep it healthy!

? **ESSENTIAL QUESTION**

Now it's time to consider and discuss the Essential Question: What does soil provide for the organisms that live in it?

WORM COMPOSTING

Earthworms have an important job recycling organic material into soil. You can watch earthworms at work with this simple worm composting jar! CAUTION: An adult needs to help with the hammer and nail.

SUPPLIES

❀ quart-sized canning jar with lid
❀ soil
❀ nail
❀ hammer
❀ worms
❀ food scraps
❀ dark construction paper
❀ tape

1 Scoop some soil into your jar. Don't pack it in tightly! The worms need room to do their work! Leave a couple of inches of space at the top of the jar. Make sure the soil is slightly damp but not completely soaked with water.

2 Have an adult poke holes in the lid of the jar with a hammer and nail. Set it aside.

3 Dig for some worms outside. You only need two or three, because there isn't a lot of space in your jar. Put the worms in your jar.

WORDS to KNOW

composting: recycling food scraps to form humus for the soil.

4 Once the worms have slithered down into the soil a little, add some food scraps to the jar. Only add things that are natural—no junk food! Tiny pieces of apple, carrot, and other types of fruit and vegetables are good worm food. You can also add small amounts of used tea leaves or coffee grounds.

Did You Know?

Worms don't have lungs. They "breathe" right through their skin! And they don't have a stomach like you do, either. A worm has one long tube running straight from its mouth all the way out its back end.

5 Put the lid on your jar and wrap the whole thing with the dark construction paper. This will give the worms the darkness they like so they'll get to work. Every few days, come back and check on your worms. Are they breaking down the food material?

6 Release the worms back outside when you're finished with this project. You can use the rich, composted soil for a plant!

THINK ABOUT IT: Did your soil change color, texture, or smell while the worms lived in it? How did it change? Why do you think gardeners use worms for composting?

WHAT DO YOU CALL IT WHEN WORMS TAKE OVER THE WORLD?
Global worming!

Just for
FUN!

17

BERLESE FUNNEL

Sneak a peek into the living world of soil! Using this funnel, sometimes called a Tullgren funnel, you can see what tiny organisms are living in a sample of soil.

1 Secure the black construction paper around the jar with tape. Set the funnel into the top of the jar.

2 Fit the small piece of mesh in the bottom of the funnel to prevent soil from falling through into your jar. Fill the funnel loosely with fresh soil.

3 Set the desk lamp so that it shines down directly on the soil in the funnel. Keep it just far enough away so it doesn't burn the soil. Soil creatures like cool darkness, so they'll move away from the light and heat.

4 Wait an hour and then take the construction paper off your jar. Are there any creatures in your jar? Use your magnifying glass or microscope to examine them. Release the creatures when you're done.

TRY THIS! Fill your Berlese funnel with soil from a different location. Try using leaf litter found at the bottom of a pile of leaves. Do the creatures you see look different? Do they behave differently? Why might different creatures thrive in different types of soil?

SOIL

SCREEN

SUPPLIES

* black construction paper
* large jar
* tape
* funnel
* small piece of mesh from an old screen or strainer
* soil or leaf litter
* desk lamp
* magnifying glass or microscope

18

CHAPTER 2
HOW SOIL WORKS

Soil does much more than simply blanket our planet and provide a habitat for plants and animals. Soil also has a role to play in the health of our planet.

SOIL LAYER CAKE

Soil is made of different layers. What if you drilled a tube straight down into the earth and lifted out a long sample core of soil? You'd see different colors in the sample, like the layers in a cake.

? ESSENTIAL QUESTION

Is all soil the same?

Each layer of soil is called a horizon. Each horizon is made of a different type of material, and is named with a letter.

ORGANIC LAYER: The organic layer, called the O layer, is what you usually see on the surface. It's made of humus and bits of grasses and other plants that haven't broken down yet. This layer can be really thick. Think of the cushy surface you walk on in a forest.

←A
←E
←B
←C
←R

The O layer can also be very thin or not even there at all, as on rocky mountaintops.

A LAYER: The A layer comes next. This is the first layer of real soil. It has organic material mixed in with mineral matter, such as bits of rocks. This is the best layer for plants and organisms to live and grow in.

E LAYER: The E layer is beneath the A layer. E stands for eluviated. This describes how materials, such as clay, minerals, and organic matter, are carried by water from the layer above it. When material moves down from the A level, it's called leaching. Together, the A and E layers make the topsoil.

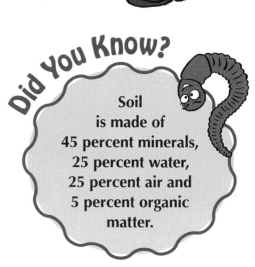

Did You Know?

Soil is made of 45 percent minerals, 25 percent water, 25 percent air and 5 percent organic matter.

B LAYER: Next is the B layer. This is called subsoil, and it's usually very rich in minerals that have leached down from the layers above it.

C LAYER: The C level is made of the parent material. This is the layer of loose rock that soil develops from.

R LAYER: Finally, there's the R level. This is the bedrock below all the soil. It includes granite, limestone, or sandstone. These are the rocks that form the parent material for some soils.

subsoil: the layer of soil below the topsoil.

water cycle: the continuous movement of water from the earth to the clouds and back to the earth again.

filter: to pass a liquid through something to remove unwanted material.

WORDS to KNOW

SOIL AT WORK

What happens when you add water to soil? Do you just get plain old mud? Water moving through soil is actually an important step in the water cycle.

Soil works hard to filter the planet's water. Have you ever watched someone cook spaghetti? When it's done you pour the contents of the pot into a strainer so the water passes through and you're left with just yummy noodles. Soil is like the strainer letting the water go through.

toxic: something that is poisonous.

environment: everything in nature, living and nonliving, including plants, animals, soil, rocks, and water.

water table: the underground water supply for the planet.

WORDS to KNOW

When it rains, the rainwater seeps into the soil. What if that rainwater had fallen on a field that had been sprayed with chemicals to kill insects? As the water moves through the soil, the soil traps many of those toxic substances that can harm the environment.

Remember the bacteria and fungi that help break down organic matter in the soil? They also help the soil get rid of chemicals and other harmful things.

Sometimes, the soil and the organisms can break down the unhealthy stuff altogether. Other times, the soil holds onto it. Through many years, if more and more chemicals are added to the soil, the chemicals can build up so much that the soil can't be used to grow anything anymore. That's when some of that toxic material gets leached back into the air or water.

Soil's ability to filter is important, because a lot of the water we drink comes from the ground. Rainwater seeps downward until it is stopped by solid rock. That place is called the water table. You can find the water table at different depths depending on where you are.

Did You Know?

The water cycle is the endless process that water travels through on Earth. It evaporates to become a gas in the clouds called water vapor. Then it condenses into liquid water to fall in the form of rain or snow. This cycle happens over and over again.

22

The water stays underground until someone taps it by drilling a well to bring the water to the surface. It can also come up naturally through a spring. A spring is a low point in the ground that touches the water table and lets the water out of the ground.

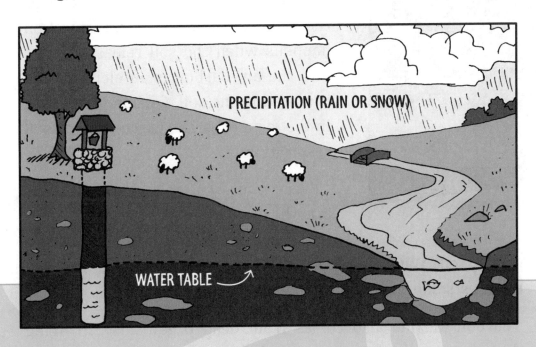

PRECIPITATION (RAIN OR SNOW)

WATER TABLE

WETLANDS

Wetlands are large areas that hold a lot of water naturally. These are really important spaces on our planet because they act as giant filters. When wetlands are destroyed, the earth loses an important resource for keeping our planet healthy.

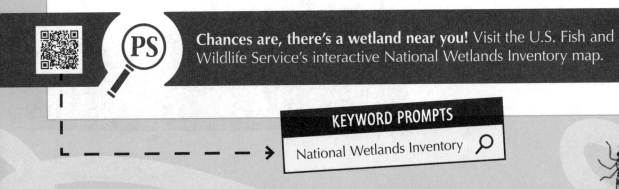

Chances are, there's a wetland near you! Visit the U.S. Fish and Wildlife Service's interactive National Wetlands Inventory map.

KEYWORD PROMPTS

National Wetlands Inventory

23

soil respiration: when carbon dioxide is released into the atmosphere from the soil.

carbon: an element found in all living things.

carbon dioxide: a gas formed by the rotting of plants and animals and when animals breathe out.

WORDS to KNOW

BREATHING SOIL

Did you know soil can breathe? It doesn't have lungs, so it doesn't breathe like you do, but soil respiration can be thought of as breathing. Soil respiration happens when the soil releases carbon into the air. Carbon is an element that is stored in the soil. Carbon is released in the form of carbon dioxide during soil respiration.

Every time you take a breath, you breathe out carbon dioxide gas. So does every animal, even the ones that live in the soil. Where does all that carbon dioxide go? The soil releases some of this carbon dioxide into the air.

Carbon dioxide also comes from dead organisms. All living things are made of carbon, so when plants and animals decay into the ground, that carbon is released into the soil. In the soil, the carbon mixes with oxygen to form carbon dioxide, which is released back into the air.

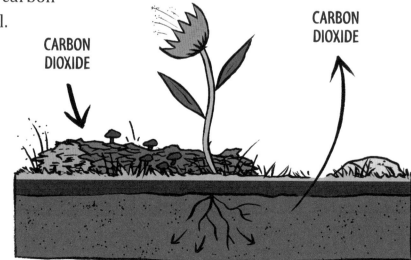

CARBON DIOXIDE

CARBON DIOXIDE

If the temperature is higher than usual, there's more soil respiration. That's not always a good thing. Too much carbon dioxide released into the air contributes to the greenhouse effect. That's when the atmosphere above the earth gets clogged with too many thick gases and acts like a greenhouse. This warms the earth's surface more and more and can contribute to climate change.

You can see that soil is a very important resource to the earth! For thousands of years, humans have learned how to use the soil in many ways, as you'll discover in the next chapter.

WORDS to KNOW

atmosphere: the blanket of air surrounding the earth.

climate change: changes to the average weather patterns in an area during a long period of time.

Did You Know?

About 10 percent of the world's carbon dioxide is stored in soil.

CARBON GOES ROUND AND ROUND

Just like the water cycle, we also have a carbon cycle. This is when carbon is released from the soil into the air, where plants breathe it in. When the plants die, they rot back into the soil, and the carbon gets released into the air again. Carbon also gets absorbed into the oceans, where ocean animals use it to make shells!

? ESSENTIAL QUESTION

Now it's time to consider and discuss the Essential Question:
Is all soil the same?

SOIL LAYERS

The soil is made of horizons stacked up like the layers in your birthday cake! You can make your own soil horizons with this easy, edible project.

SUPPLIES

❀ large, clear jar or glass bowl

❀ pudding, any flavor

❀ shelled nuts or chocolate chips

❀ rolling pin

❀ vanilla cookies, wafers, or sandwich cookies

❀ chocolate cookies

❀ shredded coconut and green food coloring

1 Spoon the pudding into the bowl or jar, keeping it piled up in the center. You don't want the pudding to hit the sides, because you don't want the pudding visible from the outside once you're done. Think of it as a core of pudding.

2 Place a layer of the nuts or chips at the bottom of the container, around the core of pudding. Be sure the nuts push up against the glass, because you do want to see them from the outside.

3 Using the rolling pin, crush the vanilla cookies until they're very fine. Set aside a small amount, then carefully pour a layer of crumbs on top of the nuts. Make sure the crumbs go up against the glass, because you want to be able to see them from the outside.

4 Crush the chocolate cookies into very fine crumbs, too. Take equal amounts of chocolate crumbs and leftover vanilla crumbs and mix them together. Then, pour a layer of this mixture on top of the vanilla crumbs in your bowl or jar. Again, make sure you can see them from the outside of the jar.

5 Pour the remaining chocolate crumbs in a layer on top, touching the sides of the bowl or jar and covering the pudding core.

6 Use the food coloring to tint the coconut green. Then sprinkle your coconut "grass" over the top of your chocolate crumbs.

THINK ABOUT IT: You should be able to see all the layers from the side of the bowl or jar. Can you identify the different horizons in your "soil"? Which food is the A layer? Which food is the B layer? What is the bedrock made out of?

GEORGE NELSON COFFEY

George Nelson Coffey was the first American to suggest that soil comes from organic materials. He started studying soil in 1900. How do you think the study of soil is different now than it was 100 years ago? What tools do scientists have that they didn't have back when George Nelson Coffey was studying soil? What do you think we know now about soil that we didn't know then?

  PS **You can view photos of George Nelson Coffey and his gravesite.**

KEYWORD PROMPTS

"George Nelson Coffey" 🔍

SOIL FILTER

When water filters down through the soil, it gets cleaned of many toxins as it moves through the different horizons. With this project, you'll see how soil can filter water.

1 Use the screen to filter the play sand. You want the sand to be as fine and clean as possible.

2 Using the toothpick, poke about five holes in the bottom of one of the large cups. Put the large cup inside one of the smaller cups. It will rest partway into the smaller cup, leaving room for liquid underneath.

3 Fill the top cup about half full with sand. Pour some of the dirty water into the top cup. What happens?

4 After a few minutes, remove the top cup and look at the water underneath. Does it look any different than before? Is it the same color?

5 Dump out the water and place the big cup back into the smaller cup.

SUPPLIES

❀ clean play sand
❀ screen or another mesh
❀ toothpick
❀ 5-ounce paper or plastic cups
❀ 3-ounce paper or plastic cups
❀ dirty water from a puddle or mix outdoor water with some soil
❀ fine soil
❀ water
❀ grape powdered drink mix

6 Next, mix together the grape drink according to the package directions. Pour some of the prepared grape drink into the top cup.

7 When it's finished dripping, remove the top cup and look at the liquid below. Is it the same color it was when you poured it in?

8 Prepare a second set of cups the same way you did the first. Poke holes in the bottom of a large cup and put it into a smaller cup.

9 Put a thin layer, about one-third of an inch, of play sand in the bottom of the large cup. Put topsoil on top of the sand until the cup is three-quarters full.

10 Pour grape drink into the top cup. Wait until it's finished dripping, then remove the top cup and look at the liquid in the bottom cup. What color is it? What does it look like? How is this second cup of filtered grape drink different from the one you poured through just sand? How do you think the soil filtered that drink? What conclusions can you make about how soil filters things such as chemicals out of water?

SOIL MOISTURE

Even though you can't see the water in soil, it's there. Soil holds on tightly to both water and air. This project will show you this is true.

1 Line the containers up in a sunny window. Leave one empty and tape a piece of black construction paper over the top of it.

2 Fill the next container half full with the moist soil from the garden. Then tape a piece of black construction paper over the top of that one.

3 Fill the last container half full with sand from the sandbox. Again, tape a piece of black construction paper over the top of it.

4 Make sure all the containers are in the sunlight for a couple of hours. Start a scientific method worksheet in your science journal. After the time is up, check the paper over each container. What do you find? Which of the papers is completely dry? Which is damp? Why is one paper more wet than another? Record your observations in your science journal.

THINK ABOUT IT: When water warms up from sitting in a puddle or swimming pool or from getting absorbed into soil, it begins to evaporate. That means it changes from a liquid to a gas. If that gas hits paper on its way into the atmosphere, it will dampen the paper. Can you explain why your construction paper was damp or dry?

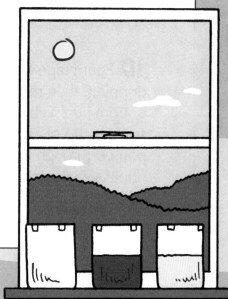

SUPPLIES

* three containers about the same size
* black construction paper
* tape
* regular soil from a garden area or other moist place
* dry sandbox sand
* science journal and pencil

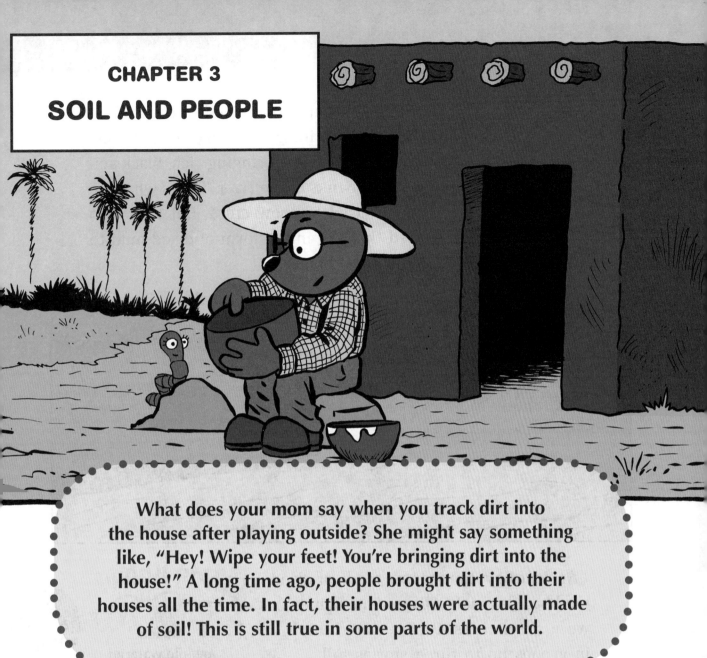

CHAPTER 3
SOIL AND PEOPLE

What does your mom say when you track dirt into the house after playing outside? She might say something like, "Hey! Wipe your feet! You're bringing dirt into the house!" A long time ago, people brought dirt into their houses all the time. In fact, their houses were actually made of soil! This is still true in some parts of the world.

In ancient times, people didn't have the same building materials we do today. They didn't have machines to help them build their homes. They had to use what was available to them when building their shelters.

ESSENTIAL QUESTION

How was soil important to people in the past?

crop: a plant grown for food and other uses.

WORDS to KNOW

Some ancient people lived in the area of the Nile River in Egypt. Every year, the Nile River would flood, bringing rich, black soil over the banks of the river. That's what the people used to grow crops. But they also used that soil in the form of dried mud to build their homes.

Ancient Egyptian houses made of dried mud had flat roofs. Some of the homes were simple huts. Others were built in groups up to three stories tall. These were the first cities, all made out of mud! Small windows in the mud walls helped keep the homes cool.

To this day, in other parts of the world such as Afghanistan, some people build their houses made of dried mud.

Did You Know?

Ancient people watered their land with a shaduf, also called a shadoof. This structure is made with a tall standing base and a pole that has a bucket on one end. You dip the bucket in the water, swing the pole around on its base, and dump the water where you want it to go.

THE ORIGINAL TABLET

Ancient people who lived thousands of years ago didn't have computers. They didn't even have paper for books. What did they use to record things? Soil, of course!

The area between the Tigris and Euphrates Rivers is called Mesopotamia. More than 5,000 years ago, the people living there created a form of writing. It didn't look like the letters you know today. It was based on pictures, called pictograms. They wrote with these pictograms on slabs of clay called tablets.

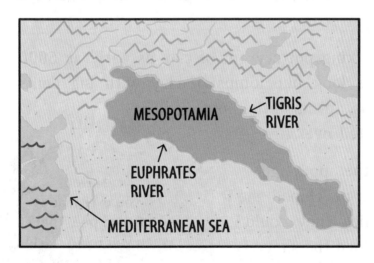

Mesopotamia: an area of ancient **civilization** between the Tigris and Euphrates Rivers in what is now called Iraq, Kuwait, and Syria.

civilization: a community of people that is advanced in art, science, and government.

pictograms: the symbols in the first written languages, based on pictures instead of letters.

cuneiform: a system of wedge-shaped letters created by ancient civilizations.

WORDS to KNOW

They rolled the clay into a flat tablet, then used a sharp stick or stone to carve pictograms into the wet clay. When it dried, the clay hardened and the tablet could be saved and shared.

Through time, people gradually changed the pictures into a letter-based script called cuneiform. These letters were wedge-shaped and became the first written language.

33

WORDS to KNOW

The clay tablets were so sturdy that many have survived more than 5,000 years. Scientists have even found some that they think were created as long ago as 3300 BCE! You can see cuneiform writing on these clay tablets.

MIX IT UP

Ancient people did more with soil than build homes and use it to write on. They also used it to make pots, plates, and cups for their food.

Humans began making pottery out of clay as early as 6000 BCE. The first pots look like lumps of clay with big dents pushed into the tops. To make the pots last, they were heated over fire.

Through time, the pots got fancier and humans developed the potter's wheel, which they could spin while they molded the shape. Before their pots dried, potters could carve patterns into the clay. Dried pottery was often painted with designs, too.

Did You Know?

Have you ever made a coiled pot? That's when you roll out a long "snake" of clay and coil it around and around on top of itself until it forms a pot. Coiled pots were very common thousands of years ago.

34

SOIL DETECTIVES

One really interesting thing that scientists do with soil is use it to solve crimes! This is called soil 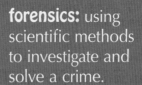 **forensics**. Special investigators use science to figure out what happened in a crime.

Because areas of soil are different, scientists can learn a lot just by examining it closely. You can, too. Try collecting bits of soil from different areas, such as the park, the beach, the forest, and your back yard. Look at the samples under a microscope or magnifying glass. Although the samples might look the same or similar when you're looking at them with just your eyes, when they're magnified they look very different.

That's because of the different **components** that make up the soil. Different soils contain different minerals and bacteria. Soils are formed differently in different climates depending on the plants that grow there and the insects that live in it. With soil forensics, it's as if investigators can see the soil's "fingerprint." Soil can give them clues about a crime. The bad guys can't beat the soil scientists!

forensics: using scientific methods to investigate and solve a crime.

component: an important part of a system or mixture.

WORDS to KNOW

AH-HA!

?

ESSENTIAL QUESTION

Now it's time to consider and discuss the Essential Question: How was soil important to people in the past?

CLAY POT

You can easily make a coil pot in the same way that ancient people did. Don't put any food in yours, though. The clay you get at craft stores isn't made to safely hold food for eating.

SUPPLIES

✿ clay that can be air-dried or baked dry
✿ plastic wrap or damp dishtowel
✿ water mister filled with water
✿ paints and paintbrush

1 Roll the clay around and squish it with your hands to soften it.

2 Break off a lump and make a flat circle about 3 inches in diameter. This is for the base of your pot. Wrap the base in plastic wrap or the damp dishtowel to keep it from drying out while you work on the rest of your pot.

3 Using a large piece of clay, roll it out into the shape of a long snake. Keep it about a half inch diameter or a little narrower.

4 Unwrap your base and lay the end of the snake around the outside of the circle. Wind the snake around and around, coiling it up on top of itself to build the sides of the pot. If you run out of snake and want your pot taller, make another snake and continue where you left off.

5 When your pot is the size you want, spray a little water on the sides and smooth the coils together to make the sides solid. You can do both the inside and the outside, or just one side of the pot, depending on how you want it to look. Be sure to seal the sides to the base.

6 To make a lid, make a circle the same size as the opening at the top of the pot. Make a handle for the lid if you'd like. Don't attach the lid permanently to the pot while it's drying, or else you'll never be able to get it open!

7 Let the pot dry according to the directions on the package of clay. When it's cool and dry, you can paint your pot.

TRY THIS! Can you think of a way to make clay pots other than making a "snake"? Ancient people kept changing and improving the ways they made things. Experiment with different methods of your own!

just for FUN!

WHAT IS A MESOPOTAMIAN'S FAVORITE AFTER-SCHOOL SNACK?
Picto-Gram Crackers!

MUD BRICKS

It would take a lot of these little bricks to build a real house, but you could probably make a nice house for an action figure with this project!

1 Put a couple of cups of soil in the bowl and start adding water a little at a time. You're making mud, but you don't want it to be so wet that it won't hold its shape. Add enough water so that it's not crumbly, but will hold its shape if you pick some up and squeeze it in your fist.

2 If you want to add food coloring, do it now and mix it together. It won't make bright colors, but it will look different from the regular soil.

3 Once you have the thickness you want, scoop the mud evenly into the ice cube tray compartments. Pack it down very tightly. If it's too loose, it won't hold its shape.

4 Let the mud dry for a few hours or overnight. Carefully flip the tray over to get your mud bricks out. Start building!

THINK ABOUT IT: Why did ancient people use mud to make their bricks? What other materials could they have used? If you were to build a home today, what materials would you use and how are they different from the ones used in the past? What natural materials could you use?

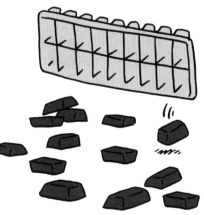

CUNEIFORM NAME

With this project, you can see what it was like for ancient people to carefully write their own names!

SUPPLIES

❀ Internet access
❀ clay that can be air-dried or baked
❀ rolling pin
❀ pencil or other pointed stick
❀ paints and paintbrush

1 Roll out a piece of clay about an inch thick.

2 Search online for a cuneiform alphabet. With the pencil carve your name into the flattened clay, using your alphabet as a guide. Traditionally, ancient people wrote up and down instead of side to side the way we do today.

KEYWORD PROMPTS

cuneiform, alphabet, images 🔍

3 Poke a hole in the top center of your tablet and let it dry according to the directions. Paint your tablet and hang your work for display!

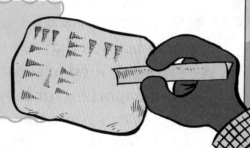

TRY THIS! Can you come up with your own alphabet? Maybe you can use simple shapes for each letter. Come up with your own "code" and write your name. Then see if a friend or family member can use your alphabet to write their name!

Did You Know?

Even school kids used cuneiform writing on clay tablets! Although learning to read and write wasn't common in ancient civilizations, some boys did get the chance to learn.

 PS

Read a lesson description and see an actual school tablet at the British Museum's website.

KEYWORD PROMPTS

cuneiform schoolwork 🔍

You've learned that soil is a resource we can't live without. We grow our food in soil and it filters our water and air. Soil is also very important for human health because both diseases and their cures can come from soil. You may think that soil wouldn't be much help to you if you got sick, but if you've ever needed a medicine called an **antibiotic**, soil has already helped you!

THE SOIL CURE

Remember, organisms called bacteria and fungi make their homes in soil. There can be good bacteria and bad bacteria, just as there can be good fungi and bad fungi.

WORDS TO KNOW

antibiotic: a substance that destroys bacteria or stops it from growing.

? ESSENTIAL QUESTION

What would happen to our health if we had no soil?

In the early 1900s, a scientist named Alexander Fleming discovered something about a soil fungus called Penicillium. It could stop a bacteria called Staphylococcus from growing and spreading in a **petri dish** in his lab. Penicillium was used to create penicillin antibiotics. Penicillin is used to fight many serious diseases, such as **pneumonia**.

petri dish: a shallow dish with a loose cover that's used to grow bacteria and other microscopic organisms in a lab for scientists to study.

pneumonia: (noo-MOW-nyuh) an infection of the lungs.

resistant: something that stands against something else.

WORDS to KNOW

Did You Know?

Scientists recently discovered a new antibiotic in soil that can kill dangerous drug-**resistant** bacteria. It's called teixobactin. Scientists are excited because there are millions of other soil bacteria species that might be disease fighters, too!

Many of the antibiotics we use today start with soil organisms. This is one reason it's important to keep soil healthy. Some scientists fear that by not taking care of the planet's soil, humans are in danger of destroying possible cures we haven't yet discovered.

root rot: when the roots of a plant rot, usually because of too much water.

WORDS to KNOW

HEALTHY PLANTS, HEALTHY HUMANS

What happens when you stay up late and eat lots of junk food? You might get sick! In the same way, soil can get sick when we treat it badly. To keep soil healthy, we shouldn't put anything into the ground or water system that kills the healthy bacteria in the soil. We should also make sure plants that are moved from one area to another are healthy in the first place so they don't spread disease.

Diseases in soil can hurt or even destroy the plants growing there. If the soil is very wet or water can't drain easily, fungi can invade plant roots and cause something called root rot. Plants with root rot turn yellow, drop their leaves, and eventually die.

 (PS) One way diseases can get into plants is through their roots, but diseases can also affect the part of the plant that's above the ground. **This video shows how this happens, and how you can help protect your garden plants.**

An overload of salt in the soil can be just as bad. Have you ever tried to shake salt out of a damp saltshaker? Salt is very good at absorbing water, even underground. If salt absorbs too much of the water in the soil, the plants won't have enough to grow.

KEYWORD PROMPTS

tomato disease barrier 🔍

Some insects and other animals living in soil are beneficial, but too many can cause damage to the plants. That's why farmers are always trying to keep a balance of critters in their crops.

Things such as gasoline and pesticides should never be just dumped into the soil. Instead, they should be disposed of properly by reading the directions on the product label.

WASH UP!

Keeping the soil healthy is an important job we all share. The food we eat depends on the soil. Do you eat fruits and vegetables? The plants that produce them grow in the soil. Even your meat depends on healthy soil because meat comes from animals that eat the plants that grow in the soil. It's important for the food chain that we are careful to prevent any diseases from starting and spreading.

Listeria is a bacteria that lives in the soil. If listeria gets into food products, it can be killed with proper handling, cleaning, and cooking. If food isn't handled properly, listeria can infect humans. In 2011, cantaloupes from Colorado were contaminated with listeria and people got sick.

pesticide: a chemical used to kill pests, such as insects.

food chain: a community of animals and plants where each is eaten by another higher up in the chain.

listeria: a bacteria that's unhealthy for animals and people.

infect: when microbes invade your body and make you sick.

contaminate: to pollute or make dirty.

WORDS to KNOW

Did You Know?

Listeria is named after Dr. Joseph Lister, an English surgeon who introduced sterilization into surgery. The mouthwash Listerine is also named after Dr. Lister.

CONTAMINATION PREVENTION

Food contamination can be prevented. The people who grow, handle, and serve food need to follow strict guidelines so that bacteria, such as listeria, don't spread. And the good news is, most of the time everyone does follow the right procedures so you stay healthy. You can help make sure you and your family can eat worry-free by following some guidelines.

* Wash fruits and vegetables under running water or scrub them with a clean produce brush before cooking, cutting, or eating them.

* Store fruits and vegetables and uncooked meats away from each other in your refrigerator so they don't touch or drip on each other.

* Wash your hands, any utensils, and cutting boards before and after handling and preparing uncooked foods.

* Clean all spills in the refrigerator and on the counters.

* Make sure the meat you eat has been completely cooked.

Because our food comes from the soil, it is a very important part of our health! Soil is also important because some cures for diseases come from microorganisms in the soil. Let's work together to make sure we have healthy soil for generations to come.

 ESSENTIAL QUESTION

Now it's time to consider and discuss the Essential Question: What would happen to our health if we had no soil?

BACTERIA FARM

Do you ever get tired of your parents saying, "Wash your hands!"? This project will help you see what happens if you don't have clean hands when you handle food.

SUPPLIES

❁ large potato or 2 small potatoes, peeled
❁ clear plastic bags
❁ marker
❁ science journal and pencil

1 First, wash your hands and your potatoes. You want to start everything out as clean as possible. If you're using a large potato, cut it into two pieces.

2 Wash your hands again. Handle one potato with your bare hands and drop it into a plastic bag. Write "clean hands" on the bag.

3 Play with your pet or go outside and play for a while. Then come back inside. Do not wash your hands! Handle the second potato and drop it in the bag. Write "dirty hands" on the bag.

4 Place both bags in a cool, dark place. Wash your hands! Start a scientific method worksheet.

5 In one week, check on the potatoes. Just look—don't touch them or take them out of the bags. What do you see? Can you spot any black, green, or white fuzzy stuff? Which potato has more?

THINK ABOUT IT: Why are there more bacteria growing on one potato than the other? If there are bacteria even on clean food, why is it okay for us to eat this food? Is all bacteria bad?

HAND-WASHING EXPERIMENT

You've seen how washing your hands can help get rid of bacteria on your skin and food. But how much hand washing is enough? Start a scientific method worksheet, then try this quick experiment to see.

1 Put a little glitter or cinnamon on your hands. Rub it around so it's spread on your skin. This is your pretend bacteria.

2 Set the timer for 30 seconds. Wash your hands with soap and water until the time is up.

3 Check your hands. Do you still have any glitter or cinnamon on them? Remember to check between your fingers and around your fingernails!

4 Set the timer for another 30 seconds and wash your hands again. Check your hands again. Keep washing your hands for 30 seconds at a time until your hands are completely clean. How long does it take? Record what you see in your science journal.

TRY THIS! Ask your parents for permission before you do this! Put glitter on your hands and, before washing, open a door with a doorknob. Have a friend or family member open the same door, then look at their hands. Is there any glitter on their hands? What does this tell you about how germs spread?

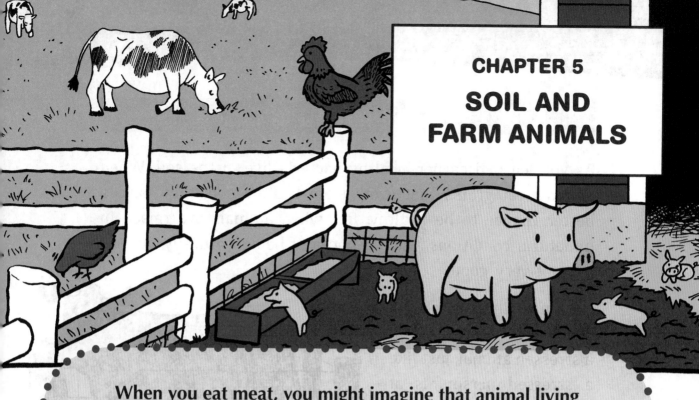

When you eat meat, you might imagine that animal living happily on a sunny farm, eating grass in the fields. Ideally, that's what farming would always look like. This kind of environment promotes healthy soil and healthy animals. Farms depend on healthy environments. Air, soil, and water are all important for producing quality **livestock** and crops to feed people.

As the world's population grows, the majority of people don't raise their own food anymore. Large food companies make more and more of our products. Many of these companies turn to commercial farming. That's when animals are raised in controlled and often uncomfortable areas such as cages or very tight pens.

WORDS to KNOW

livestock: animals raised for food and other products.

commercial: large businesses that produce large quantities of something.

? ESSENTIAL QUESTION

How does the health of farm animals affect you and your family?

47

BACTERIA FIGHT BACK

As you learned earlier, healthy bacteria live in the soil. When animals eat grains that grow from healthy soil, they have a better chance to be healthy. But when animals are raised in unnatural conditions, their chances of being naturally healthy are not very good.

Animals in uncomfortable living conditions are stressed. And a stressed animal, just like a stressed person, is at greater risk of getting sick. Large commercial farmers often give their livestock antibiotics to prevent the animals from getting sick.

One problem with giving animals antibiotics is they cause problems farther down the food chain. All animals naturally have good and bad bacteria in their intestines. When animals are given antibiotics, it kills most of those bacteria. But some bacteria successfully fight and survive. Then those bacteria go on to multiply, and all the new bacteria are resistant to the antibiotic. That means the antibiotic doesn't work on the new bacteria.

WHY SHOULDN'T YOU TELL SECRETS ON A FARM?
Because the potatoes have eyes
and the corn has ears!

just for FUN!

When animals with these resistant bacteria become food for humans, some of those bacteria are passed along to the people eating the food. If those people get sick, antibiotics that should help them get better don't work, because those bacteria have already "learned" how to fight off the antibiotic!

LIFE ON A FARM

organic farming: raising livestock and crops in a natural way.

graze: to eat grass.

rooting: when pigs push around the soil with their snouts.

WORDS to KNOW

Some farmers try to keep things as natural as possible by practicing organic farming. Organic livestock are fed a natural, healthy diet. They have access to fields where they are free to walk around and graze. These animals aren't given drugs unless they're sick. Once they are given antibiotics, they can't be called organic for a certain period of time. Sometimes, organic farmers might wait too long to treat sick animals. This can be one of the problems of organic farming.

On healthy farms, animals are allowed to roam a fenced area of land called a pasture or range. They are not crowded in. Cattle will graze on the grasses and plants. Pigs like to dig their snouts into the ground and push around in the soil, called rooting. And chickens scratch at the soil, pecking around for insects. They often give themselves dust baths to clean their feathers and help prevent insects from clinging to their bodies.

SNORT! SNORT!

Animals have an impact on their pastures when they graze and root around. So it's healthiest for the soil if they regularly rotate to different pastures. That gives the soil a chance to replace its nutrients naturally through time and helps maintain a healthy environment.

MAGNIFICENT MANURE

If you've ever seen animals in a field, you've definitely seen lumpy piles of manure all over, too. That manure is very important to keeping the soil healthy!

When animals such as cows and horses eat grains and grasses, their bodies take in some of the nutrients from what they've eaten. The rest gets pooped out onto the ground. Slowly, the soil absorbs the nutrients in the manure. These nutrients are important for healthy plants to grow.

Sometimes people with gardens but no animals will buy manure to spread on their plants for that reason. Manure also increases the carbon in the soil, which is an important source of energy for plants.

Did You Know?

One horse can produce 35 to 50 pounds of manure every day. A cow produces about 65 pounds each day. Cows can poop up to 15 times every day!

50

THE FIRST COMPOST

In ancient Rome, Marcus Cato, also known as Cato the Elder, was one of the first people to talk about using manure to improve the soil. He made the first recorded reference to what we now call compost.

PS You can see a picture of ancient youth gathering olives from olive trees on the surface of this pot.

KEYWORD PROMPTS

Amphora olive gathering 🔍

Another benefit of manure is that it helps make the soil a good consistency. Sandy soils can use manure to help hold in moisture that would otherwise run off. Manure helps prevent the leaching of nutrients. Tight soils, such as those with a lot of clay, can be loosened up a bit with manure so plants can push their roots into it.

THE SOIL FOOD WEB

Food chains are everywhere in nature. That's when, for example, a grasshopper eats grass. Then a frog eats the grasshopper, and a snake eats the frog, and an eagle eats the snake. Each species eats an organism from the group below it to form a food chain.

Many food chains combine into a food web. Sunlight and rain give plants the energy and fuel they need to grow. The bacteria in the soil help plants grow, too. The microscopic organisms in soil feed the small creatures, which feed the larger creatures. The creatures return to the soil when they die and rot, feeding the bacteria that help the plants.

Farm animals benefit by feeding on these healthy plants. Then they deposit their manure to return nutrients to the soil to keep the web going.

Soil is at the bottom of the food web, but it's critical to life on Earth. Without soil, we'd have no plants and no animals.

? ESSENTIAL QUESTION

Now it's time to consider and discuss the Essential Question:
How does the health of farm animals affect you and your family?

COW PATTIES

Serve these edible "cow pies" and tell your friends and family about how manure helps the soil!

SUPPLIES

❀ microwave

❀ bowl and mixing spoon

❀ 2 cups chocolate chips

❀ 1 tablespoon shortening

❀ 1 cup mix-ins: raisins, almonds, or crispy cereal

❀ waxed paper

❀ candy corn

❀ chocolate cookies

❀ shredded coconut

❀ green food coloring

1 In the microwave, melt the chocolate chips and shortening together in the bowl. Keep checking and stirring—you don't want to burn your cow pies. The mixture should be very smooth.

2 Stir in your mix-ins. Drop the melted mixture into circular piles on the waxed paper. Gently press in some candy corn. Let the cow pies harden in the refrigerator for two hours.

3 Crush the chocolate cookies and spread them out on a plate. This is your "soil."

4 Put the coconut in a plastic bag. Squirt in a couple drops of green food coloring, and shake it until the color is mixed through. Shake your coconut grass out onto your crushed cookies and set the cow pies on top. Share with your friends and family!

THINK ABOUT IT: What would be different on a farm if cows ate different food? How would their manure or "cow patties" be different, and how would that affect the soil?

SOIL BACTERIA CREATION

There are thousands of different kinds of bacteria in a single spoonful of soil. If you were to look at them under a microscope, you'd see they each had different shapes. With this game, you can create your own "bacteria"!

SUPPLIES

❀ science journal
❀ colored pencils
❀ dice
❀ paper or cardstock

1 Draw a grid in your science journal with seven rows and six columns. This is going to be your master game list.

2 Label your grid. Start with the example below or make your own.

Number rolled	Color	Body shape	Body	Extras	Pattern
1	Blue	Oval	One part	Bumpy	Solid color
2	Red	Circle	Two parts	Many strings	Stripes
3	Yellow	Triangle	Three parts	One string	Dots
4	Green	Long	Tiny	Spikes	Zigzags
5	Black	Short	Large	Smooth	Stripes and dots
6	Orange	Fat	Squiggly	Bristles	X marks

THIOSPIRILLUM

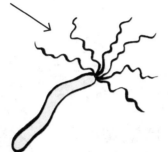

PROTEUS

STAPHYLOCOCCUS

NITROGEN-
FEEDING
BACTERIA

Did You Know?

Bacteria are super tough. They can live almost anywhere—in near-boiling water to inside rocks and ice! There are even some bacteria that can live on radioactive waste. Now that's tough!

3 Each player takes a turn rolling the die. For each turn, players add the trait that matches the number they roll from the next column in the sequence. For example, if you roll a three on your first turn, your bacteria will be yellow. If you roll a one on your second turn, your bacteria will be oval shaped. Draw your bacteria. Who has the funniest looking one?

THINK ABOUT IT: Why do bacteria come in different shapes? What do you know about the shapes of other living things, such as dogs? A dachshund is shaped very differently from a greyhound. What can each of them do differently? Does this help you think of reasons bacteria have different shapes and features?

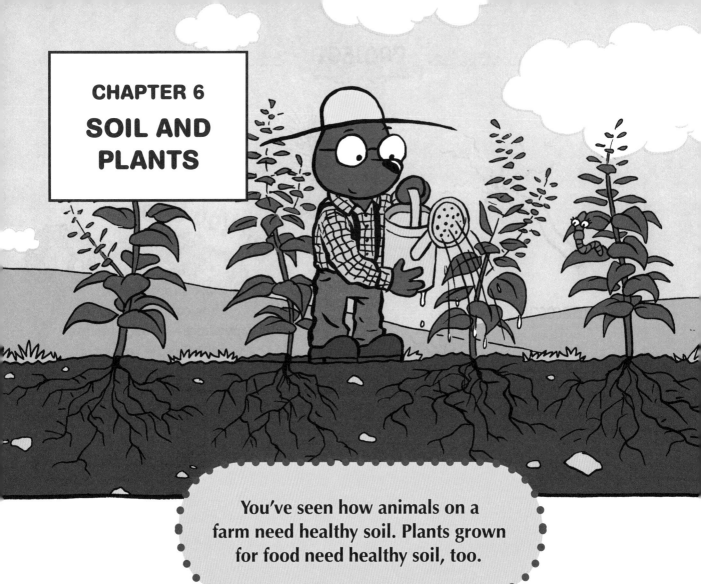

CHAPTER 6

SOIL AND PLANTS

You've seen how animals on a farm need healthy soil. Plants grown for food need healthy soil, too.

Remember how soil is made partly of tiny bits of rock? These bits have come from bigger rocks that have been broken down by ice, wind, and water.

Rocks are made of minerals. When they're broken down through time, they add the minerals to the soil. These minerals are nutrients that are important to help living things grow and thrive.

? ESSENTIAL QUESTION

How does weather cause the earth to change? How does this change the soil?

START WITH A SEED

Plants start with seeds. Have you ever planted a garden? If so, you know that the seeds for different plants look different. Some seeds are large and flat, others are tiny and round. Some you can actually eat, such as sunflower seeds. No matter how different they look, all seeds work the same way.

To plant, you bury a seed in the soil. When it rains, moisture seeps through the soil and softens the skin of the seed. The seed swells a little bit and splits open. Then the seed begins to grow. The root pushes down into the soil while the shoot pushes up in the other direction, toward the surface.

Once that shoot breaks through the surface of the soil, it runs out of its own energy. That's when the sun takes over. It shines on the seedling and gives it the energy it needs to keep growing into a full-sized plant.

Did You Know?

Earthworms were wiped out in North America during the Ice Age. They only came back when they hitched a ride on the ships of European settlers during the 1600s.

WORDS to KNOW

Ice Age: a period of time when ice covered a large part of the earth.

ALL TOGETHER NOW

You've seen how the soil is full of living organisms, all working together to keep the soil healthy. These organisms help plants, too. Underground creatures, such as earthworms, create tiny tunnels in the soil. They push the soil around near the roots of the plant, and help the air and water work their way through the soil to the plant.

PLANT POWER!

When you look at seedlings, they look pretty fragile. But they're actually fairly tough. As long as there is soil, sunlight, air, and water, they go to work getting stronger every day.

Plants are helping the soil, too. When the soil is wet, plants draw water out of the soil through their roots. Some roots help break up rocks over time, which makes even more soil. Plants and their root systems also help hold soil in one spot. When nothing anchors soil down, wind or water blows it away or washes it away in a process called erosion.

WORDS to KNOW

erosion: the gradual wearing away of rock or soil by water and wind.

Back in the 1930s, people in the United States discovered how important plants are to prevent erosion. Farmers on the prairies overworked the land. They plowed up the soil and planted crops that needed a lot of rain.

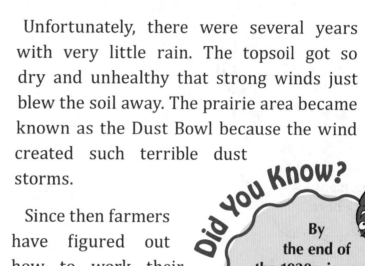

Unfortunately, there were several years with very little rain. The topsoil got so dry and unhealthy that strong winds just blew the soil away. The prairie area became known as the Dust Bowl because the wind created such terrible dust storms.

Since then farmers have figured out how to work their land in ways that help prevent it from drying out. This keeps the soil healthy and rich.

Did You Know?

By the end of the 1930s, in some areas, more than 75 percent of the topsoil had been blown away.

(PS) It's hard to imagine the size of the dust storms that destroyed the prairies, but you can see actual videos of them.

KEYWORD PROMPTS

1930s great dust storm 🔍

IT'S IN THERE

Plants depend on many different nutrients to grow. Some of these, such as hydrogen, carbon, and oxygen, come from the air and water. These help plants in a process called photosynthesis. This is when a plant changes sunlight, water, and carbon dioxide into the energy it needs to grow.

Plants get mineral nutrients from the soil. These include nitrogen, potassium, calcium, and iron. Do you take a multi-vitamin every day? If you look at the bottle, you'll see some of these same nutrients you need to grow, too! Since plants can't get them from taking vitamins, they depend on the soil to provide them.

Did You Know?

Just one shovel scoop of soil has more living things in it than all the humans ever born.

TIME FOR YOUR VITAMIN!

?

If the soil is healthy, then the plants will grow strong. To be healthy, though, farmers can't plant the same crops in the same place year after year. There need to be plenty of helpful organisms and nutrients in the soil. Nutrients can be added to the soil to enrich it and help plants grow.

? ESSENTIAL QUESTION

Now it's time to consider and discuss the Essential Question: How does weather cause the earth to change? How does this change the soil?

FLOWER POWER

With this experiment, you can see how water and nutrients are pulled up through the roots of a plant. Start a scientific method worksheet.

SUPPLIES

* 1 empty water bottle for each flower
* water
* food coloring
* freshly cut white carnations
* scissors
* science journal and pencil

1 Remove the labels from the water bottles so you can see inside the bottles easily. Fill each bottle about one-third full of water.

2 Add about 15 drops of color to the water, one color per bottle.

3 Cut the end of each carnation's stem at an angle. Place one in each bottle.

4 Put your flowers in a sunny spot and come back a few hours later to check on them. Don't worry if you don't see a change! Keep checking at least twice a day for several days. Record your observations in your science journal.

WHAT'S HAPPENING? Since the flowers are cut, they no longer have roots to pull nutrients and water from the surrounding soil. But they continue to draw water up through their stems, bringing the food coloring along with it. When the water evaporates from the petals and leaves of the flowers, the dye is left behind, coloring your flowers.

DRINK UP!

Sometimes weather conditions aren't perfect for plants. How much water do plants really need to thrive? By controlling how much water several different plants get, this experiment will help you find out.

SUPPLIES

- ❀ several containers for plants, such as paper cups or small pots
- ❀ potting soil
- ❀ bean or sunflower seeds
- ❀ science journal and pencil
- ❀ ruler
- ❀ water
- ❀ measuring cup

1 Put the same amount of potting soil and plant seeds at the same depth in each container. Try to keep all conditions the same for each pot, including a sunny spot to watch them grow.

2 Start a scientific method worksheet. Make a chart with a row for each plant. Across the top, put the dates on which you measure each plant's growth.

3 Give each plant the same amount of water, but change how often you water each plant. For example, water Plant A twice a day. Water Plant B every day, Plant C every other day, and Plant D every third day.

4 When seedlings start to poke up from each container, start measuring them and marking it on your chart. What do you find? Does one plant do better than the others? What is the difference in the way the plants look? Is one greener or taller? What does that tell you about plants and water?

ROOT WINDOW

Have you ever wondered what it looks like when the roots start pushing down from a sprouting seed? With this project, you'll be able to sneak a peek!

1 Carefully wet the paper towel, squeeze out the excess water, and flatten it into a square that fits in the plastic bag. You want the paper towel wet, but not dripping.

2 Put the wet paper towel into your plastic bag, keeping it flat. Carefully place several seeds on the middle between the plastic and paper towel. Using the water dropper, add a couple more drops of water to the paper towel near the seeds. You don't need to close the bag.

3 Tape the bag to a sunny window so the seeds face the glass.

4 In two days, check on your seeds. If the paper towel is drying out, add some drops of water. What do you see? Check on your seeds every day. What's happening? Record your observations in your science journal. Make sure the paper towel stays damp.

5 When the roots are long, you can take the seeds out and transplant them into soil.

THINK ABOUT IT: Why can seeds sprout without soil? How long can a plant grow without soil?

SUPPLIES

* paper towel
* clear plastic zip bag
* radish or sunflower seeds
* water dropper
* tape
* science journal and pencil

SUPPLIES

- ✿ small container
- ✿ potting soil
- ✿ bean seeds
- ✿ toothpicks
- ✿ penny
- ✿ science journal and pencil

PENNY POWER

It's hard to believe a tiny seedling is very strong. But if it's grown in healthy soil with proper sunlight and water, it can be pretty powerful! After all, it's got to push through the soil and break through the surface. Here's a fun project to see just how strong those plants can be.

1 Fill the container with soil. Gently press a small hole into the soil about 1 inch deep in the middle of the container. Drop in a seed. Cover with soil and lightly water until the soil is damp but not soaking wet. Place your container in a sunny spot.

2 When the seedling pokes through the soil, press four toothpicks into the soil to form a square around the place you planted the seed. Push them into the soil about halfway.

3 Gently place a penny inside your toothpick square, using the toothpicks as guides to hold the penny in place. Your penny will be resting on top of your plant.

4 Continue caring for your plant. What happens? How strong is your plant? Record your observations in your science journal.

CHAPTER 7
DANGERS TO SOIL

You might not think that something such as soil could ever be in danger. After all, the soil itself isn't alive. It can't get burned or ripped up. But, as you've learned, soil contains living organisms and nutrients and is a vital part of the web of life. It is possible to put soil in danger.

WHERE DID THE SOIL GO?

We've learned about soil erosion. This is when the top layers of soil are washed or blown away by wind or water. Erosion is a major danger to soil that can be caused by the actions of people. Do you remember the Dust Bowl?

? ESSENTIAL QUESTION

How important is soil as a natural resource?

65

You know that plant roots help hold soil in place. If people remove all the trees and other plants from an area, the soil isn't held in place anymore. The more exposed the soil, the more likely it is to be carried off by wind and water. Are there a lot of storms where you live? Those storms could hurt the soil.

When soil erodes, that area loses most of its nutrient-rich layer. People who try to plant anything there won't have much luck because the quality of the soil won't be good anymore.

WHY DID THE FARMER PLANT LIGHT BULBS?
He wanted to grow a power plant!

just for FUN!

EASTER ISLAND

You may have heard about the enormous rock statues on Easter Island in the South Pacific. Some scientists and historians believe that the people of Easter Island caused erosion problems for themselves. They cut down the few trees that were on the island and over-worked the land. Because of significant erosion, the inhabitants couldn't plant enough crops to survive. Half of the native plants died out because they couldn't grow any more.

(PS) **You can see pictures of Easter Island here.** Does it look like a good place for farming?

KEYWORD PROMPTS
Easter Island Britannica 🔍

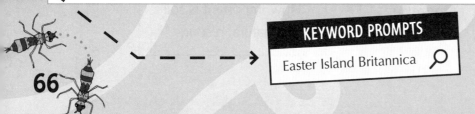

RUN, RUN, RUN

With erosion comes another problem, called runoff. Because the quality of eroded soil is so poor, farmers might add artificial fertilizers and pesticides to try to help their crops. But when it rains, some of those chemicals get swept away, along with the soil, into the water table.

This leads to water pollution that affects drinking water and the ecosystems of lakes and wetlands. Fish and wildlife can get sick and die.

With erosion, there is also an increased danger of flooding. When it rains and there's no soil to soak up and filter the water, the water often ends up rushing into rivers and overflowing the banks.

runoff: when fertilizers and pesticides leach out of the soil and into the water system.

fertilizer: any substance put on land to help crops grow better.

ecosystem: a community of living and nonliving things and their environment. Living things are plants, animals, and insects. Nonliving things are soil, rocks, and water.

WORDS to KNOW

NO DUMPING!

Another threat to soil is contamination. That's when manmade chemicals or other pollutants get into the soil. This upsets the balance of nutrients and organisms there. Soil contamination can happen at factories and farms or when people dispose of certain kinds of waste by dumping it on the ground. Using containers that aren't able to hold waste properly also contaminates the soil.

Not only can plants get sick and die from soil contamination, people are affected by it, too. Do you remember the water table? It's below the layers of soil. As contaminants move downward, they can end up in our drinking water, which makes people sick. Contaminants often don't break down quickly, so they stay in the environment for a very, very long time.

Did You Know?

Recycling a ton of paper spares 17 trees. Recycling half of the world's paper would save 20 million acres of forest. All those trees help stop erosion, and at the same time they clean the air through photosynthesis.

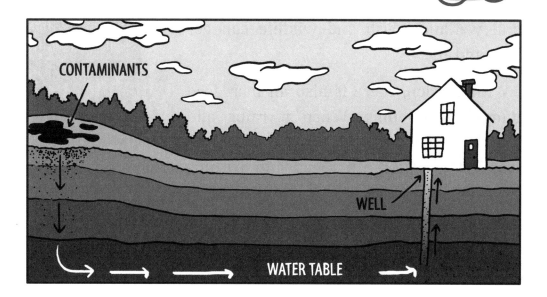

CONTAMINANTS

WELL

WATER TABLE

WASHED UP

So what does it all mean? Why should we be concerned about the dangers to soil? If the soil is destroyed, our ability to grow food for ourselves becomes limited. After all, if you don't have healthy soil, you can't plant crops! There are more than 7 billion people on the planet relying on soil for food.

CLIMATE CHANGE

Many scientists also warn that the loss of topsoil contributes to global warming and climate change. Global warming is the slow rise in the planet's average temperature. This happens partly because fewer plants growing means that less carbon dioxide is absorbed from the atmosphere. More carbon dioxide traps more heat. Just like in a greenhouse, the surface air gets warmer because of all that trapped heat. Higher global temperatures change the climate.

HEAT AND LIGHT

SOME HEAT ESCAPES INTO SPACE

EARTH

ATMOSPHERE

CARBON DIOXIDE AND OTHER GREENHOUSE GASSES TRAP HEAT IN THE ATMOSPHERE

Soil might be in danger from human actions, but there is plenty that you can do to help make sure it stays healthy! Learn what you can do in the next chapter.

? ESSENTIAL QUESTION

Now it's time to consider and discuss the Essential Question: How important is soil as a natural resource?

SUPPLIES

* scissors
* 3 plastic milk jugs
* 3 plastic water bottles
* wooden board long enough to hold the milk jugs side by side
* books or rolled-up towels
* soil
* grass seed
* water
* rocks and leaf litter
* string

SOIL RUNOFF EXPLORATION

This project requires you to grow some plants in advance, but it's a fantastic way to really see the effects of soil runoff. Be sure to have an adult help you with the cutting!

1 Lay each plastic milk jug on its side and have an adult cut a section away as shown below. Have an adult cut the plastic water bottles in half across the middle, so the top with the cap is in one piece.

2 Take one jug and fill it with soil. Plant plenty of grass seed in it and cover the seed with a layer of soil according to the directions on the package. Put this in a sunny place and water every day or two until you have a full container of growing grass.

3 Put the board in a sunny place and prop it at an angle using the books or rolled towels underneath. You want the higher side of the board near the window, so it tilts away from the sun.

4 Put the milk jugs on their sides on the board with the open cut side facing up and the spout open pointing slightly down.

PROJECT

5 Use the string to tie the tops of the water bottles so they hang just beneath the spouts of each jug. Any runoff is going to drip into these water bottle tops, so be sure they're lined up right! You might want to put an old rag or towel on the floor underneath in case there's any splashing.

6 Now you need to prepare the remaining two jugs. The first jug will already have the grass you planted. In the second jug, add a mixture of soil, rocks, and leaf litter. In the last jug, just put plain soil. You'll end up with three jugs: One with grass, one with a mixture of material, and one with plain soil.

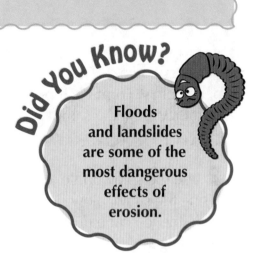

Did You Know?

Floods and landslides are some of the most dangerous effects of erosion.

7 Each day, water the containers. Make sure to pour the water in one spot every time, toward the back, away from each milk jug's spout.

WHAT'S HAPPENING? Watch what happens through time. Look at the color of the water in each of the small water bottles. Which one is clearest? Why? What's the difference between the jug with the growing grass and the one with bare soil? You can see how much more material ends up in the water bottle without anything to anchor the soil.

SUPPLIES

❁ 3 shallow pans or trays
❁ books or folded towels
❁ soil
❁ spray bottle with water
❁ straw
❁ ice cube
❁ science journal and pencil

EROSION STUDY

In nature, wind and rain contribute to erosion. Even the ice in glaciers push the earth around! With this experiment, you can see for yourself the impact of the weather on erosion. Start a scientific method worksheet.

1 Prop one end of each tray up slightly with the books or folded towels. Pile some slightly damp soil at the end of each tray. Form each pile into a little mound, making sure they're all the same height.

2 Use the spray bottle to squirt one pile with water five times. Using the straw, blow puffs of air on the second pile five times. Slide the ice cube down the third pile five times using a pencil or your finger.

3 What happened to each pile? Is one more affected by "erosion"? Repeat all the steps again and record the results in your science journal. Does one erosion method work faster than another?

4 Keep repeating the steps until you've eroded most of the soil in the pans. Notice which pan eroded fastest and which the slowest.

TRY THIS! Find places in your own community that have been impacted by soil erosion. What are people doing to try to stop the erosion? Sometimes little walls or barriers can help keep the soil in place or planting trees or bushes can help keep the soil from eroding.

You can help save our soil! Everyone can. If everyone works together, the soil can be protected so it continues to be a vital part of our environment and food web.

EAT LOCAL!

When you hear people say they are "eating local," what does that mean? Are they munching on street signs? No! "Eating local" means buying food from stores and restaurants that get their meat and eggs and fruit and vegetables from nearby farms.

ESSENTIAL QUESTION

Why should soil be saved or conserved?

Almost all local farms are small. Commercial farms are large and produce a lot of food. They often use chemicals and farming practices that harm the soil. Remember what you learned about animals that are kept in small spaces on commercial farms? It's unhealthy for the animals and the soil. Small farms are less likely to practice the kind of farming that damages the soil.

Small, local farms are more likely to use growing techniques that promote healthy soil. When you buy from local farmers, you help keep local families in business. And you help keep the soil happy!

Did You Know?

Composting improves the soil. It also helps you reduce the amount of trash your family creates.

COMPOSTING

Another way to help the soil is to recycle food scraps by composting them. Potato peels, orange peels, egg shells, and apple cores are all food scraps. What about the leftover peas that you leave on your plate?

Everyone throws away some food. How much food does your family throw away each day? Imagine how much food is thrown away every day in the whole country!

Composting is a way of recycling organic material such as leaves, food scraps, and grass clippings. Through weeks and months the organic material breaks down into humus that can be added to the soil.

The organic material has nutrients in it. Farmers and other people with gardens mix the humus into the soil to enrich it and return nutrients back into the ground.

COMPOST

SOIL-FREE

We can take care of the soil by not using it as much. But how can we do this if we are trying to grow more and more food around the world? Scientists are trying to help soil by thinking of ways to grow plants without using soil at all!

Hydroponics is one way. Plants are grown in something other than soil, such as gravel, wood fibers, or even sand. The nutrients that plants usually get from the soil still have to be delivered. Sometimes those nutrients are sprayed right on the plant's roots.

Another way of growing plants without soil is with aeroponics. That's when plants are suspended in the air without any kind of growing material at all. Then, nutrients and water are both sprayed on their root systems.

Using hydroponics and aeroponics, the farm of the future might look very different.

WHAT CAN YOU DO?

Even people who aren't farmers or scientists can make a difference. Here are some things you can do to help save the soil.

* Do you have a garden? Pull the weeds up by hand so your parents won't have to use harmful chemicals to kill them.

* Shop for organic produce from local farmers at the grocery store or at a farmer's market near you.

* Be sure your family doesn't pour leftover or used chemicals or oil onto the soil. These contaminants can ruin the soil, seep into the water supply, or run off into other bodies of water and harm the environment.

* Help your neighborhood plant a community garden. This reduces how much you have to buy from stores.

* Make a simple window garden to grow small plants to eat, such as herbs or lettuce.

By working together, we can save a precious natural resource and make our own lives healthier. Save the soil!

Did You Know?

There is 40 percent less soil erosion in America today compared to the 1990s. That's partly because of the work people are doing to save the soil.

? ESSENTIAL QUESTION

It's time to consider and discuss the Essential Question:
Why should soil be saved or conserved?

COMPOST CONTAINER

If you want to compost food scraps, you need a good container. CAUTION: Ask an adult to cut the bottle for you.

1 Rinse out the bottle and screw the cap on very tight. Remove any labels. Have an adult cut the bottle about a third of the way down, but not all the way around the whole bottle. You will want the bottle to flip open.

2 Flip the bottle open and place a layer of soil on the bottom of the bottle. Use the water to moisten the soil, but don't get it soaking wet. Add a thin layer of natural food scraps, such as fruit and vegetable scraps. Add a little layer of leaves and more soil. Keep alternating layers until the bottle is almost full. Flip the bottle closed and tape it shut.

3 Set your bottle in a sunny place. If you notice little beads of water on the top of the bottle, open the bottle cap to let it dry out a little. If the contents of the bottle look dry, sprinkle a little water on them.

4 Once a day, roll the bottle to mix it up. After about a month, check on the contents of your bottle. If everything looks dark brown and crumbly, it's ready for the garden!

TRY THIS! Create a larger bin outside and compost your food scraps every day. Toss in some soil now and then and mix it with a shovel. Remember, meat should never go into a compost pile and you need to enclose it to keep animals out.

SUPPLIES

- clear 2-liter bottle
- knife or scissors
- soil
- water
- food scraps
- leaves
- tape

PIZZA GARDEN

Gardening and growing food is fun on its own, but creating a pizza garden is even more fun! You can grow herbs such as Greek oregano, sweet basil, Italian parsley, and rosemary, as well as Georgia sweet onions, Roma tomatoes, and bell peppers.

When you create a garden that has everything you need to make a pizza, you're helping the soil by paying attention and caring for that spot in your yard. Plus, you're not buying pizza that has ingredients from a commercial farm. It also tastes fresher and better!

SUPPLIES

✿ sunny spot in your yard with healthy soil

✿ edging, such as wood scraps or rocks, to divide your garden

✿ compost

✿ seedlings of herbs, onions, tomatoes, and bell peppers

✿ water

1 Plan your garden layout. If you have room, make a circular garden that looks like a pizza!

2 Using the edging, section your garden into parts, one for each plant you'll be growing.

3 If you have compost, mix it with the soil to give your garden the healthiest start.

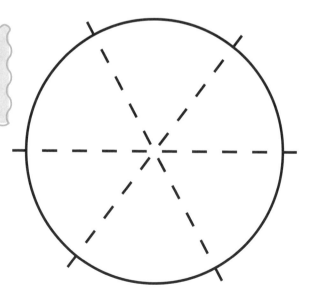

4 Plant the seedlings. Use the chart on the following page to figure out how much space you should leave between plants.

Plant	Space between seedlings
Herbs	15 to 18 inches
Bell peppers	12 to 15 inches
Onions	4 to 5 inches
Tomatoes	at least 2 feet

5 Water your garden regularly and keep an eye out for anything that's growing that isn't one of your seedlings. These are probably weeds. You can just pluck them out with your hands—no chemicals necessary!

6 When your tomatoes and bell peppers get taller, ask an adult to help you make a cage to keep them from falling over.

7 When your harvest is ready, pick your produce and have a pizza party!

THINK ABOUT IT: What other meals can you think of that you can grow most of the ingredients for? How about some vegetarian meals?

SUPPLIES

❀ a way to contact your community members, such as an online message board or bulletin board

❀ paper

COMMUNITY GARDEN

You might want a garden, but don't have any room to grow one. Maybe other people in your community want one, too! If you plan a community garden, you provide a fun activity for your community and also help the soil. You'll need an adult to help you with this.

1 Find out if enough people want to participate. Use the community contact list, or put up a flyer in your library or other community board. Ask if anyone is interested, and have them contact an adult who's helping you out.

Ask everyone:

- Are they interested in a community vegetable or flower garden?

- Will they be able to volunteer their time, tools, and supplies?

2 Try to get a local business to sponsor you. Create a flyer and ask an adult to give it to local businesses. Sponsors sometimes donate land near their business, or they may contribute tools or other supplies. Some businesses that might be interested are health food stores, churches, schools, senior citizen groups, or food coops.

3 When you have the space and some interested community members, choose a name for your garden.

4 To prepare the site, get everyone together to pitch in and clear the area. You may want to plant bushes, flowers, or put up a little fence so other people will be aware it's a community space.

5 If everyone is going to have their own plot, decide how you're going to section the garden up and label the areas. Otherwise, everyone can be responsible for the whole thing together. Also, decide if everyone's going to bring their own tools when they take a turn working the garden or if you're going to lock everything up in one place and give everyone a key.

6 Consider putting up a rain-proof bulletin board so everyone can easily communicate with everyone else. Even just a sturdy stick with paper inside a sheet protector taped shut will work. With an adult's permission, you can create an online group so everyone can communicate that way, too.

TRY THIS! Plan a community dinner made from produce grown in the community garden!

You can watch a short video about what it's like to be a part of a community garden.

KEYWORD PROMPTS

Brighton Hove community garden video 🔍

SOIL-FREE GARDEN

What else can plants grow in besides soil? With this experiment, you might discover the new way to feed the planet!

SUPPLIES

❀ several containers for plants, such as paper cups or small pots

❀ materials other than soil to grow plants in, such as sand, fine gravel, bits of sponge, torn up fabric, or cotton

❀ bean or pea seedlings, about an inch tall

❀ small sticks

❀ water

❀ ruler

❀ science journal and pencil

1 Put one type of material in each of your containers.

2 Gently loosen all the seedlings except one from where they're planted. Carefully rinse off any compost or soil from their roots. Keep the one plant in its original container with the compost or soil it was grown in. This will let you compare all the other materials to the original.

3 Plant one seedling in each container, being careful to tuck them in so they're supported by the material. You may need to prop the plant up with a pencil or small stick.

4 Gently water each plant, and place all your plants in the same spot. This will ensure that they all get the same amount of sunlight and warmth.

5 Start a scientific method worksheet in your science journal. Make a chart with a row for each type of material you used. Across the top, put the dates on which you measure each plant's growth. What do you think will happen in each pot?

6 Using the ruler, measure each plant and write the measurement down on your paper. Every couple of days, come back and measure each plant and write down the measurement. If any of the growing substances are dry, add a little water.

7 After a couple weeks, look at your results. Which plants grew best? Which didn't grow at all? Is there any difference in the way they look? Is one more yellow or maybe larger than the others? What can you tell about whether the materials you chose would make good substitutes for soil? How can you give your plants nutrients without soil and without chemicals?

THINK ABOUT IT: What does this activity show you about the challenges of growing food without soil? What is hard about it? What works really well? Do you think we'll ever grow the majority of our food without soil?

SOIL MAD LIB

**Use the parts of speech and as many glossary words
as you can to fill in the blanks and complete this silly story!**

✳ **noun:** a person, place, or thing.

✳ **plural noun:** more than one person, place, or thing.

✳ **adjective:** a word that describes a noun.

✳ **verb:** an action word.

✳ **adverb:** a word that describes a verb. Many adverbs end in -ly.

Party Pooper!

There was once a worm named ——————, who lived in ————. She
　　　　　　　　　　　　　　　NAME　　　　　　　　　　　PLACE

would crawl through the soil with her friend, ——————. One day, she found
　　　　　　　　　　　　　　　　　　　ANOTHER NAME

a —————— buried in the soil. She tried to crawl around it, but it was
　　NOUN

very ————.
　　ADJECTIVE

So she and her friend decided to make it their home. They invited their friends, a

————, a ————, and —————————— for a party. One of their friends
ANIMAL　　　ANIMAL　　　　CARTOON CHARACTER

was a very ———— ————. When he arrived, he brought ———— and
　　　　　ADVERB　　ANIMAL　　　　　　　　　　　FOOD

————————.
TYPE OF DRINK

They were enjoying their party, when a farmer started planting ———————— right
　　　　　　　　　　　　　　　　　　　　　　　　TYPE OF PLANT

over her home! The farmer watered his crop with ———————— and used a
　　　　　　　　　　　　　　　　　　　TYPE OF LIQUID

———— to pull his plow. The ———— party members all started
ANIMAL　　　　　　　ADJECTIVE

———————— and ———————— because they thought their ————
VERB ENDING IN –ING　　　VERB ENDING IN –ING　　　　　　　　　　ADJECTIVE

house was being destroyed. But when the farmer saw their party, he stopped

planting and decided to join them instead!

Glossary

A

acidic: describes a substance that is low on the pH scale and loses hydrogen in water. Examples of acidic substances include lemon juice and vinegar.

aeroponics: a method of growing plants without any soil or substitute material.

antibiotic: a substance that destroys bacteria or stops it from growing.

atmosphere: the blanket of air surrounding the earth.

B

bacteria: tiny organisms found in animals, plants, soil, and water.

basic: describes a substance that is high on the pH scale and gains hydrogen in water. Examples of basic substances include soap, baking soda, and ammonia.

BCE: put after a date, BCE stands for Before Common Era and counts years down to zero. CE stands for Common Era and counts years up from zero. The year this book was published is 2015 CE.

bedrock: the layer of solid rock under soil.

C

carbon: an element found in all living things.

carbon dioxide: a gas formed by the rotting of plants and animals and when animals breathe out.

cell: the smallest, most basic part of a living thing.

chemical: the pure form of a substance. It has certain features that can react with other substances. Some chemicals can be combined or broken up to create new chemicals.

civilization: a community of people that is advanced in art, science, and government.

climate change: changes to the average weather patterns in an area during a long period of time.

commercial: large businesses that produce large quantities of something.

component: an important part of a system or mixture.

composting: recycling food scraps to form humus for the soil.

contaminate: to pollute or make dirty.

crop: a plant grown for food and other uses.

cuneiform: a system of wedge-shaped letters created by ancient civilizations.

Glossary

D

decay: to break down and rot.

E

ecosystem: a community of living and nonliving things and their environment. Living things are plants, animals, and insects. Nonliving things are soil, rocks, and water.

element: a pure substance that can't be broken down, such as hydrogen, oxygen, carbon, or gold.

eluviate: when materials move down through the soil to the layer below.

environment: everything in nature, living and nonliving, including plants, animals, soil, rocks, and water.

erosion: the gradual wearing away of rock or soil by water and wind.

expand: to spread out and take up more space.

F

fertilizer: any substance put on land to help crops grow better.

filter: to pass a liquid through something to remove unwanted material.

food chain: a community of animals and plants where each is eaten by another higher up in the chain.

forensics: using scientific methods to investigate and solve a crime.

fungi: organisms that grow on and feed on rotting things.

G

gravity: the force that pulls things down toward the surface of the earth.

graze: to eat grass.

H

habitat: a plant or animal's home.

horizon: a layer of soil.

humus: soil formed from decaying leaves and organisms.

hydrogen: the most common element in the universe. Hydrogen and oxygen are the two elements in water.

hydroponics: a method of growing plants in a material other than soil.

I

Ice Age: a period of time when ice covered a large part of the earth.

infect: when microbes invade your body and make you sick.

inorganic: not living.

L

landscape: a large area of land with specific features.

leaching: when minerals and other matter move out of the topsoil.

listeria: a bacteria that's unhealthy for animals and people.

livestock: animals raised for food and other products.

M

mammal: a warm-blooded animal, such as a human, dog, or cat, that can keep itself warm. Mammals feed milk to their young and usually have hair or fur covering most of their skin.

manure: animal waste.

Mesopotamia: an area of ancient civilization between the Tigris and Euphrates Rivers in what is now called Iraq, Kuwait, and Syria.

microbe: a tiny living or nonliving thing. Bacteria and fungi are living microbes that are also called microorganisms.

microscopic: something so small that it can be seen only with a microscope.

minerals: nutrients found in rocks and soil.

N

natural resource: something from nature that people can use in some way, such as water, stone, and wood.

nutrients: substances in food, soil, and air that living things need to live and grow.

O

organic matter: rotting plants and animals that give soil its nutrients.

organic: something that is or was living.

organic farming: raising livestock and crops in a natural way.

organism: a living thing.

P

parent material: material that eventually becomes soil, such as rock.

particle: a tiny piece of matter.

pesticide: a chemical used to kill pests, such as insects.

petri dish: a shallow dish with a loose cover that's used to grow bacteria and other microscopic organisms in a lab for scientists to study.

Glossary

photosynthesis: the process in which plants use sunlight, water, and carbon dioxide to create energy.

pH: the scale people use to measure how acidic or basic something is.

pictograms: the symbols in the first written languages, based on pictures instead of letters.

pneumonia: (noo-MOW-nyuh) an infection of the lungs.

R

resistant: something that stands against something else.

rooting: when pigs push around the soil with their snouts.

root rot: when the roots of a plant rot, usually because of too much water.

runoff: when fertilizers and pesticides leach out of the soil and into the water system.

S

silt: particles of fine soil, rich in nutrients.

soil: the top layer of the earth, in which plants grow.

soil respiration: when carbon dioxide is released into the atmosphere from the soil.

species: a group of plants or animals that are related and look like each other.

subsoil: the layer of soil below the topsoil.

substance: the material that something is made of.

T

topsoil: the top layer of soil.

toxic: something that is poisonous.

tropics: the area near the equator. This is the imaginary line around the earth halfway between the North and South Poles.

W

water cycle: the continuous movement of water from the earth to the clouds and back to the earth again.

water table: the underground water supply for the planet.

METRIC CONVERSIONS

Use this chart to find the metric equivalents to the English measurements in this book. If you need to know a half measurement, divide by two. If you need to know twice the measurement, multiply by two. How do you find a quarter measurement? How do you find three times the measurement?

English	Metric
1 inch	2.5 centimeters
1 foot	30.5 centimeters
1 yard	0.9 meter
1 mile	1.6 kilometers
1 pound	0.5 kilogram
1 teaspoon	5 milliliters
1 tablespoon	15 milliliters
1 cup	237 milliliters

BOOKS

Soil Basics, Capstone Press, 2011, by Mari Schuh

Soil, Bellwether Media, 2014, by Chris Bowman

Why Do We Need Soil?, Crabtree Publishing, 2014, by Kelley Macaulay

Seed Soil Sun, Boyds Mills Press, 2012, by Cris Peterson

WEBSITES

Soil 4 Kids: www.soils4kids.org

Geography and Geology for Kids: www.kidsgeo.com

Soil Biological Communities for Kids: www.blm.gov/nstc/soil/Kids

Soil Science Society: www.soils.org

Soil Association: www.soilassociation.org

Resources

QR CODE INDEX

ESSENTIAL QUESTIONS

Chapter 1: What does soil provide for the organisms that live in it?

Chapter 2: Is all soil the same?

Chapter 3: How was soil important to people in the past?

Chapter 4: What would happen to our health if we had no soil?

Chapter 5: How does the health of farm animals affect you and your family?

Chapter 6: How does weather cause the earth to change?
How does this change the soil?

Chapter 7: How important is soil as a natural resource?

Chapter 8: Why should soil be saved or conserved?

Index